FAMILY SECRETS

Enjoy!

Ann Sims

Family Secrets

a memoir in verse

Ann Sims

Wicker Press

Revised Edition 2001

Library of Congress Control Number: 96-92672

ISBN: 1-57502-315-6

Cover Design by
Lorrayne Harris

Photography by Meg Pryor

Proceeds will be given to mental health associations, & local charity bazaars.

Additional copies are available. For your convenience, an order form can be found at the back of this book.

Printed in the United States by:
Morris Publishing
3212 East Highway 30
Kearney, NE 68847
1-800-650-7888

For Our Grandchildren

Sonya, Justin,
Sarah and Brandon

Contents

Wings

Shadow

Letting Go

Family Recipes

"It is possible that when we travel deep enough, we always encounter an element of sadness, for full awareness of ourselves always includes the knowledge of our own ephemerality and the passage of time. But it is only in that knowledge—not in its denial—that things gain their true dimensions, and we begin to feel the simplicity of being alive. It is only that knowledge that is large enough to cradle a tenderness for everything that is always to be lost—a tenderness for each of our moments, for others and the world."

Eva Hoffman,
Lost in Translation.

Butterfly Wings

Family Secrets is a scrapbook of family snapshots, beginning with a 1913 wedding in a small mining camp. In Bessemer, Alabama, where the Holomon family made their home for 57 years, our father died at age 94 after our parents were married 64 years. Four years later, in Jacksonville, Florida, the passing of our mother at age 86 brought the era of *Family Secrets* to a close.

Growing up in a traditional southern family with a sister ten years and a brother seven years my senior, I knew no abuse. Our parents took pride that the three of us graduated from college, were happily married, and that two of us were blessed with children and grandchildren. We lived a protected life, but...

A general shimmering of daily life springs from the simple abundance of secrets hidden in the most ordinary family—if we examine the drama as a child ponders a butterfly's wing.

Unlike other books of poetry, for best enjoyment read *Family Secrets* from front to back. It tells a story.

* * *

Acknowledgments

Grateful acknowledgment is made to the following publications for permission to reprint poems in this volume:

Publication	**Poem**
Alive Now!	Sunday Service
Golden Times	Mam's House
	First Beau
	Old Gray Felt Hat
	Who's Reddest
	"Say Your Little Piece"
Kalliope	Epilogue
	Details
Mobius	Family Secrets
	Father And Son
Poet	Letting Go
	Monkeyshines
Skylight	Close Harmony
State Street Review	Ain't Dead Yet
	Broke
	Like A Day Lily
	Cornelia's Return
	Gentle Women 1942
	Closet Confession
	Surprise
	Call Of The Woods
	First Beau
	Green Christmas
Stet	Old Patterns, 1913
Treasure House	Father, Feeble
Verve	Like Old Times

I am grateful to First Coast Writers' Festival for awarding prizes to: "Ain't Dead Yet," "Broke" and "Like a Day Lily."

Special Thanks To

Mal Sims, my beloved
who carefully read and reread each piece.

Dr. Mary Byron, my poetry professor
who inspired the work.

My fellow bards
for many helpful suggestions.

My older sister, Margaret,
who fed me family stories
from before I was born
and beyond.

The Family

1913-1981

Mama	Hazel Thomas Holomon
Daddy	Walter Strong Holomon (Honey)
Older Sister	Margaret Holomon Page
Older Brother	Walter Holomon (Buddy)
Younger Sister	Ann Thompson Holomon Sims (Me)
Margaret's husband	Ellis Page
Buddy's Wife	Fran Holomon
Ann's Husband	Malcolm (Mal) Sims
Mal's Grandmother	Mam Foster
Ann's Paternal Grandmother	Ann Thompson Holomon
Her Paternal Grandfather	Grandpa Holomon
Her Maternal Grandfather	Papa Bill Thomas
Her Maternal Aunts and Uncle	Luckie Meagher Mildred Bankston Buster Thomas

Mama's Stories

Wind Wanderings

When Mama listens
to wind wanderings,
her eyes glow
with knowings
deeper than oak roots.

Long black hair glowing,
long scarlet skirt blowing,
naked feet scampering
over gangly grasses
like leaves in the breeze.

When she roams river meadows
feasting on wild berries,
their juices tickle her chin.

She reaches out to
tree frogs,
and tree creepers.
Chirping chickadees
encircle her.

Instincts pure
as sun's radiance
dappling through trees,
her head's in the wind,
feet attuned
to earth's core.

Mama! Mama!
God's metaphor.

Mama As A Girl

I'm my papa's girl.
My mama sits in her
bedroom,
shades pulled down,
crying.

My papa is mining
superintendent.
Saturday nights
he comes in singing loud.
(Good thing the horse knows
how to trot the buggy
home.)

I'm Papa's girl.
He built me a doll house,
brought me baby rabbits
got me a baby sister.
I push her every day
in her little buggy.

When I'm grown up
I won't
sit in my bedroom,
shades pulled down,
crying.

Bessie Mines
in Maben, Alabama

Mama As A Bride

The mining camp was abuzz.
The young ladies all ogled
the handsome six-footer.

My papa had hired
Mr. Holomon as timekeeper
for the office in Bessie Mines.

Black folks spied us girls
flirting with this newcomer,
"The doctor's girl,
got the purty face,
but Miss Hazel,
the superintendent's girl
she sho 'nuff got the figger."

I'd rather have the figure.
In my cinch-waisted dress,
long black hair piled high,
I caught Mr. Holomon, thirty one
and me only eighteen.

He left our church wedding
wearing a black bowler hat.
I felt such pride—
Mr. Holomon at my side.

Walter and Hazel Holomon
Married in Maben, Alabama
1913-1977

Old Patterns

Mama searched her pattern drawer
as she reminisced,
"After the wedding
I couldn't keep calling
your daddy Mr. Holomon,
but I just couldn't
call him Walter.

"So I called him Honey.
Your Aunt Luckie called him Honey.
Your Aunt Mildred called him Honey.
Your Uncle Buster too.
Honey was his name."

Like a bee searching for nectar
Mama flitted
from pattern to pattern,
until she found one marked
in a loose loving scrawl—

Honey's nightshirt.

Bessemer, Alabama

Can't Be!

Mama was shocked at the news:
Lying in bed with her firstborn,
she learned her mother was pregnant.
"Can't be! she said.
Five months after her Baby Margaret,
Mom's little sister, Mildred, was born.

It's A Boy!

Margaret watched Grandpa Holomon
rocking and singing
"Bye-O-Baby" to Buddy.
Grandpa's eyes were gleaming—
so tickled to have that grandson
to carry on the family name.

Three and pretty,
ribbon in her hair,
Margaret hid behind the door,
than sank sobbing to the floor.
"Mama," she wept, "why
can't I carry on Grandpa's name?"

Bessie Mines

A Day Lily

As a bride
Mama met Grandmother Ann,
admired her spirit,
but never saw
her once-lovely face.
Family members knocked
before entering,
giving Grandmother time
to pull her sunbonnet low.

It covered her countenance
like a day lily's closed petals
protecting the center
after the bloom.
It hid ravages wrought
on her cheeks, nose and lips
by the hot dragon-breath
of primitive X-rays.

A day lily
does not survive the night.
Death,
the ultimate healer,
swept her away
like a gentle autumn breeze,

leaving me her name.

Birmingham, Alabama, 1914

A Miss

I figured I must be
something special
since the Lord
had to intervene
to get me here.

"No, we didn't plan this one,"
Mama was quick to add,
"but the Lord sure
knew what he was doing
when he sent us Ann.

"To my disappointment
and Honey's delight,
only ten months after our wedding
Margaret was born.
I wanted a year's honeymoon.

"Since Mrs. Davis, next door,
whispered to me
the latest preventions,
Buddy didn't arrive
for three years.

"Even with no help from Honey,
I got good at preventions.
But with a little girl ten
and a little boy seven
something went amiss.

"We named her Ann."

Born in Maben, Alabama, 1924

"Say Your Little Piece"

When company dropped in
they'd say,
"Mr. Holomon,
that's a mighty pretty
little girl
you've got there."

Daddy would say,
"Well, she's just as pretty inside
as she is outside."

Mama would smile.
"Ann, say your little speech
for the company."

With grand gestures:
"I'm a cute little girl
with a cute little figure,
but stand back boys
till I get a little bigger."

Bessemer, Alabama, 1928

Dartmouth Avenue

Mama's Day

A porch
stretched across the front
of our Alabama home.
Gnarled oak trees lined
Dartmouth Avenue.

In the cool of the morning,
Mama did her house work,
put on her apron
cooked greens and cornbread—
Dad came home to dinner
at the stroke of noon.

After he left
for his afternoon's office work,
she took a lazy bath,
a twenty-minute nap,
then dressed
to sit on the front porch.

Wearing the cool
blue dotted-swiss frock
she had made,
Mama looked fresh
as the morning glories
growing over the back fence.

She rocked on the porch
in her green wicker rocker,
sipping ice tea,
fanning a Wonder Bread
cardboard-fan-on-a-stick,
waiting for a neighbor
to drop by and sit a spell.
"I do believe I smell rain."
she said.

I miss the front porches
of that old neighborhood,
the pink blooming dogwood,
the gentle folk
of my childhood.

Wicker Rocker Song

Mama hummed while she was rocking
In her high-back wicker chair,
And her lullabies slid off-key
As she cuddled Margaret there.

Margaret grew up. Ellis kissed her
On the creaky wicker swing.
Honey bees buzzed in magnolias.
Ellis gave a diamond ring.

Underneath the flower pot, at night
The door key was left waiting
While the breeze caressed the ivy
And moonlight hugged the railing.

Now one year after the wedding
Mama's rocker's still awhirl,
Rocking one more generation—
Margaret's wrinkled baby girl.

Auntie's Wedding

Does one's earliest memory
have a special meaning?
At four
I'm auntie's flower girl
wearing the pink silk dress
my mama made.

In ivory satin shorts,
the comely little ring bearer,
like a palomino pony,
balks at going down the aisle,
while I obediently
toss my rose petals.

After the wedding,
Oh, how mean!
Why, why do they throw
rice at my auntie!

Tears wash my cheeks
and almost reach
my silky dress
when a princely groomsman
hearing my cries,
gathers me in his arms.

What does this first memory
foretell?
A raging river of tears
to cross?
Will a gentle man
forever hold me in his arms?

Montgomery, Alabama, 1928

A Taste Of Springtime

Heaven is under our feet
as well as over our heads.
Thoreau

I knew springtime had come
when I could go
barefoot.

My feet were tender
trapped all winter in oxfords
and Sunday Mary-Janes.

On the bank of the creek
I squashed mud between my toes
and bathed my feet in cool waters.

The hillside was wild
with Johnny-jump-ups, maidenhair,
and yellow buttercups.

Tucked away like timid children,
lavender violets hid
among the woodsy smells.

I skirted an anthill
and ducked a bumblebee
as I darted across the mossy earth—

shoeless
breathless
long hair flying.

Winter was a time of hot chocolate
and marshmallows toasted by the fire,
but it was the taste of springtime

I would always remember.

Warmth Of Fire

Fred's Fine Furniture
delivered our first radio—
a Majestic mahogany console,
and a box of Whitman's
Sampler for us kids.

Daddy opened the red
Prince Albert Canister,
dipping the bowl of his
crooked neck pipe,
fingers curled round it
packing shreds,
adding a pinch,
lighting-and-drawing
and lighting-and-drawing.

He leaned his head back
on his old leather chair
as he listened
to Paul Whitman's music.

Munching chocolates,
we kids gathered round
the new Majestic,
the warmth of the fire,
and Daddy.

1929

The Mirror

Daddy was one
to let events unravel
like a ball of yarn
in the paws of a playful kitten.

Thirteen years his junior
Mama never ceased
to amaze and amuse him.

She declared,
"If his big Morris chair in the den
is surrounded by his smoking stand,
hard candy, newspaper and radio.
he pays no attention
to the rest of the house.
When I think of making a change
his pat answer is that things look
just fine
the way they are."

One day she asked,
"Honey, will you hang this mirror
in the living room for me?"

"Things look just fine
the way they are," he said,
"The nail for that heavy mirror
will make a heck-of-a-hole.
Soon you'll fancy something else
and down will come the mirror."

He dutifully hung the mirror.
And, in a matter of months
his prediction came true.
However, Mama was too proud
to ask him
to take down the living room mirror.

She secretly did it herself,
each day barely beating the noon deadline
when Daddy returned home for lunch.
Mending the gaping hole
for four mornings she painted
like a hummingbird in flight
until the living room walls
were covered by a heavenly aquamarine.

Pulling off a stunt
with the cunning of a sorceress
was too delicious a secret to keep.
Weeks after the completed job she said,
"Honey, I've a secret to tell you."

He lowered his paper,
filled his pipe
while raising one eyebrow,
"Is it about the mirror?"

Who's Reddest

I'm brought up almost
as an only child.
I listen with envy
to Margaret's and Buddy's tales
of their childhood—
together.

Margaret says to him,
"Remember when we begged Daddy
to take us hunting?"

"Yeah," Buddy nodded his head.
"He warned we couldn't keep up.
Then he allowed us to get lost
in the deep woods
not returning until
the hoot owls began to hoooot!"

Margaret interrupts
"Remember when we borrowed
Daddy's hammer to make
that tree house,
then lost the hammer?"

"Oh, those three days
he gave us to find it—
before the spankings.
You always made me go first."

Margaret adds,
"Then we compared bottoms
to see who's reddest."

My Sister Margaret

Mama beams while Ann practices
her scales, like she's some day
gonna make us famous
as a concert pianist.

When Buddy and I are lucky
to find good radio music,
we practice dancing together.
Ann is drawn to the piano
like a world famous artist.

As if tossing aside
a pebble in his path,
Buddy lifts Ann
from the piano bench,
drops her on the floor
with a thud.
"Now stay there, Dinky."
Next come Ann's screams,
"Maaamaaa!"

Mama comes bustling in,
wiping her hands on her apron.
"Son, stop it. You don't realize
your strength!"

As she returns to the kitchen
she mumbles, "Lawsy mercy.
If it weren't for me
they'd kill her for sure."

Margaret Grows Up

I was always too young.
I entered high school
at twelve,
wearing corrective shoes.

At my girlie
spend the night parties,
we had to keep down
our squeals and giggles
so we wouldn't wake
my baby sister. Ann was two.

I borrowed tuition monies,
interest free,
from our rich Aunt Jean,
who lived on Miami Beach.

Though I entered college
at only 16, I relished
my college classes.
I realized I was pretty
when the beaus began to call.

Dreaming

She's sixteen, I'm six.
Margaret leaves
for Alabama College
in her flapper dress
and bobbed hair.

She returns
wise and wonderful.
She's excited about
The Great Gatsby
by F. Scott Fitzgerald,

I dream
of growing up,
flying away to college,
returning wise and wonderful.

The Eldest

Even in her eighties
Margaret squeals with delight
over a big win at cards,
reads the latest books,
wears dazzling colors,
and burns candles
around her whirlpool bath
while she luxuriates.

We sisters spend hours
on the phone
recalling family secrets.
Yesterday I said to her,
"Margaret, being oldest,
you got our parents broken in.
There was less discipline."

"They were determined to make me
perfect," she said.
By the time they finished with me
they were exhausted! So they doted
on you like a couple of godparents.

Closet Confession

Clothes poles
in Mama's walk-in closet
are just the right height—
I swing to my fall
pole-clothes-and-all.

Buried in Mama's dresses,
covered with fright,
I want to run outside
and hide.
Tear-stained but dogged
I face her.

"You come
telling the truth."
She pulls my tousled self
to her bosom.
I inhale the fragrance
of her lavender bouquet.

For All Those Years

On January sixth
my neighbor, Margaret Ann
dropped by to see me
and said, "How old are you,
Ann?"

"Five."

"I'm seven. I'm two years
older than you."

"I'll be six tomorrow.
You're just a year and a day
older."

Margaret Ann was taller than I.
She drew herself to her full
height and said,

"I'm seven. You're only five."

Iron Men

Carousel! Ferris Wheel!
Puffy Cotton Candy!

For my seventh birthday
Daddy took Margaret Ann and me
to the Alabama State Fair.
Our shaggy hair tangled
in the wind
as we whirled
on the roller coaster.

We promised
if we got lost
to return
to Vulcan-The-Iron-Man.
I looked up
to his giant hands.

Today Vulcan stands
like a lighted steeple
atop Shades Mountain,
overlooking
former iron ore mines,
former fiery blast furnaces.

He overlooks the majesty
of the red-clay
hills, valleys,
the grandeur
of the giant forests
of The Magic City.

But Daddy
overlooks
the world.

Birmingham, Alabama

The Chin

Me in back seat,
Mama and Daddy riding
in front, she asked,

"Honey, don't you think
Margaret's best feature
is her eyes?"

"Mama, what's
my best feature?"

Looking over her shoulder,
"Your chin"

I spent days
viewing it
from all angles.

Family Secrets, 1930

Daddy rarely lost
his temper.
One morning he flung
a white-starched shirt
across the kitchen floor.
Button missing!

He slammed the back door
as he left for work.
Mama's eyes misted
with anger and hurt.

She confided,
"And that's not all.
He uses cuss words
at the office.
Your brother told me so."

Mama trusted me
with family secrets.

After Daddy Hired Ladies

curse words
at the office
were no more.

Mama said
"It's a blessing—
young women
pampering him
making his work
easier."

But when Daddy brought home
daisies which M'Lou gave him
as a thank-you
for his office rides,
the posies flew
from Mama's hands
into the waste basket.

Daddy's laughter filled the room
but he never
drove M'Lou again.

Buttered Cornbread

All those years
Mama cooked
hot rolls, biscuits or cornbread
for every meal.

Whistling down the hall
sitting down to supper
resting bowed head
on folded hands, Daddy prayed,

"Good Lord we are thankful
for these and all
Thy many blessings. Amen"

One day, with sideways glance, Mama said,
"Next man I marry
won't be getting
hot breads every meal.
No siree-bob!"

Daddy buttered his cornbread.

Sunday Service

Mama watched
Old Mr. Keaton, with hearing aid
push his wife's wheel chair
beside their customary pew.

He laid an opened hymnal
across her twisted hands,
before each hymn.

Mama looked into her doll-eyes
then turned to him saying,
"How's Mrs. Keaton today?"

"Oh she's okay,"
he said proud and plain.

Mama later said,
"I think of his
Monday through Saturday
service."

Carols

Green Christmas

At ten, I try to remember
my Sunday School lesson,
"It is more blessed..."

Peggy lives next door.
Being a year older,
I can do things better
and I'm prettier too.

I like Peggy (an only child)
except at Christmas—This year
she got a bedroom filled with white
French Provincial furniture!

I return from Peggy's
knowing my green eyes have seen
the Green Ghost of Christmas.

1935

Surprise

A symbol
of my femininity—
tiny face and numerals,
dainty gold links.

Christmas eve I hear
Mama, Margaret and Buddy
giggling in the back room
(knowing I'll be surprised!)

Buddy brings out
a huge gift box
laying it under the tree
like a heavy block of gold.
What a clever way
to wrap a watch!

Next morning I unwrap
a rust-colored rayon
store-bought-dress.

1936

Silent Night Holy Night

Baptist or not
at Christmas
we have eggnog.

Mama whips cream,
Daddy pours Four Roses,
Aunt Mildred puts on
her drunk act
to Uncle Red's
thigh-slapping grin.

Margaret, Buddy, all
singing melody.
Me singing alto
to Daddy's bass.

Everyone in harmony.

Bessemer, Alabama, 1938

Crutches

When Daddy spoke
we listened.

Guests arriving
for Christmas dinner
found
Daddy in the living room,
crutches at his side.

Mama says,
"Last night
he stumbled
over a chair."

Wide eyes rivet
on Baptist Deacon Daddy,
"Well I do declare."

"I was drunk"
Daddy smoked his pipe.

My eyes widened.
I had never known him to drink
anything but Christmas eggnog.

I looked on him with pride.
Any other man
would have said nothing.

1937

Cornelia's Return, 1948

After cleaning Mama's house
(waiting to do dinner dishes)
Cornelia sneaked naps
under the guest room bed.

When Cornelia and I
were teenagers
my washed, starched
crimson hand-me-downs
looked just right
on her slim ebony body.

She left Alabama
for Detroit.
Years later at Christmas
Cornelia returned to call.

On the winding drive,
following Cornelia
like twin cherubs
in starched winged pinafores,
toddled
Sheila Ann and Sharon Ann

my namesakes.

Wings

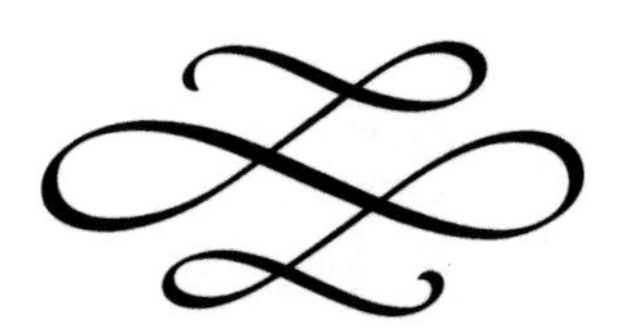

Den Of Lions

The first issue of *Life Magazine*
arrived at our home the year I turned
twelve. In full color, a wet newborn
adorned the cover. "The Birth of a Baby,"
the feature pictorial story,
left me in awe.
Medical experts applauded the magazine,
but *Life* was banned in thirty three cities.

The editor was arrested!
If he'd had the opportunity,
Baptist Deacon Daddy
would have done the job himself.
He helped "Doc" bring each of us
into the world, but he was firm
in protecting the innocence of his girls.
He limited Margaret's dating.

"Before sixteen," he said,
"it's like throwing her to a den of lions."
Later Mama said, with a twinkle in her eye,
"Well now. Before we met, maybe your dad
was a young lion himself."
After Daddy's and Mama's comments,
I wondered at what age I would be allowed
to mix and mingle with the lions.

Loving Cup

The tall master of ceremonies
pronounced, "And the winner is...
Miss Ann Holomon."
He lifted me,
twirled me around and around
in my red net off-shoulder gown,
as the orchestra played
"You Must Have Been
A Beautiful Baby.."

Spots lights winked.
Applause serenaded Miss Bessmer,
crowned at 15.
Silver loving cup whispered
that this magic moment
was the beginning of a new era,
as though a prince had awakened
her with a kiss.

Sally Rand's Fan Dance

Buddy is driving our family
from his Georgetown graduation
to the N.Y. World's Fair.
I'm a bobby soxer: full skirt,
saddle shoes and whoopee socks.

Nearing Flushing Meadows,
our Chevy's brakes go out,
so Buddy maneuvers thru crushing
traffic, using gears and hand brake.

Billy Rose's spectacular Aquacade
stars Eleanor Holm along with
glamorous precision swimmers
in a water ballet. Unforgettable!

Then comes the shocker: the world
famous sensational Sally Rand.
I can't believe our whole family
will be watching such goings-on.

I guess Dad figures we're grown up—
Margaret safely married,
Buddy soon a Marine officer,
and I am *sweet sixteen.*

This dazzling dancer lady
swings and sways huge fans
and we see so little skin!
But we keep peeking around....
The thought she might drop one
stirs our imaginations.

1940

Coming Of Age

My most memorable
rite of passage
was Buddy's return
from college.

He didn't call me Dinky.
We had long talks.
Once we even double dated.
He gave me tips
on how to play
the dating game.

As ever, he was my hero.
During the war,
I liked to believe
I was his heroine. He wrote,
"From one battle to the next,
I carry your framed portrait.
I tell the guys, 'Say, Mister,
That's my little kid sister.' "

First Beau

John was always there.
When we were twelve
he saved lunch money
for Monday matinees
where we held hands.

He had nickels left
for ice cream cones
at Stull's Bakery—
then we talked
as he walked me home.

John was always there.
When we were sixteen
he finagled his dad's Buick
to take me to Birmingham
to see Bogie in Casablanca.

At Grayson's Ice Cream Shop
he emptied his pockets of change
for me to spend as I chose.
John was always there—
until I married Mal.

Cobblestones

I took the bus from Buddy's
Georgetown graduation
to June Week at Annapolis
and Midshipman Jimmy.

Mama had made each dancing
net-skirt-layer
a delicious tint—
lemon
raspberry
apricot
swirling
and twirling
like
sherbet
ripple.

I dreamed
of Annapolis cobblestones
leading to romance.

But Jimmie married
my neighbor—
his heart belonged
to Margaret Ann.

Annapolis, Maryland, 1940

"You Was Robbed"

Southern towns and beauty contests
went together like babies
and Ivory Soap.

Reading *The Birmingham News*
I turned pink with excitement—
"The lucky girl selected
to represent Alabama in Atlantic City
will end her tour in Hollywood
for screen tests at MGM."

"Hollywood?" Daddy barked.
You're enrolled at Judson College."
Over the Miss America crown
Daddy favored the sheepskin.

Life Magazine called
old Judson college (1838)
"the school for gentle women."
I was bored of being a gentle woman.

About the Miss Alabama Contest,
Daddy didn't say yes
but he didn't say no.
Glancing at his face
as I left for Preliminaries,
I felt like a girl running away
to join the circus.
Gentle Southern women
are wild at heart.

On the night of Finals
at the ornate Alabama Theatre
I swept to the piano to play
"In the Mood"
"Syncopated Cow-Cow-Boogie."

Accompanied by the band
I sang to blinding spotlights
"Ain't misbehavin'
I'm savin' my love
for yoooou."

My older sister was with me,
my parents absent.
I longed to see Daddy's face beam
like when I sang "Holy, Holy, Holy"
from the choir loft of Highland Baptist.

Next morning, through tear-smudged mascara
I looked at the photos in *The News*.
"Running a close second was Ann Holomon
beautiful and gifted young musician
who was presented a silver loving cup."

Drying my sniffles,
I received a fan letter
from a Pvt. Hal Howard
written with pencil
in a large scrawl—
"You was robbed!"

1942

Broke

Goodbye to the nest:
Alabama's Judson college
school for gentlewomen.

Spreading my wings
with American Airlines
in New York City.

Dancing at the Waldorf
with West Point cadet.
Partying
with a Broadway cast.

Automats for dinner.
Buying fruit-lunches from
Toni the vendor
who won with the horse
Alabama.

Owing for uniforms.
Scrimping for a trousseau.

Waiting
for high school sweetheart
returning from war
to take me home

broke.

New York City, 1945

Wings

On a blind date
in a Piper Cub
he flew me high
in the sky.

War clouds gathered.
Leaving for the Air Corps
he gave me a bracelet—
wings engraved.
My name misspelled.

One World War
and two I-do's later
we flew
from Highland Baptist,
my bridal veil
like snowy egret wings
quivering.

As a bride,
I couldn't know
that fifty years later
he'd be my anchor
as well as my wings.

1941-1945

Rio Or New York?

"Hello Ann? Meet me in Miami!
I'm flying up from Rio and
I've reserved rooms at the Versailles."

I'm packing for stewardess school
at the Big City. It starts in three days.
"I'll get you there in time," Mal said.
"Now I'm stationed in Rio! What a spot
for a honeymoon at government expense."

We met at the Versailles, a Miami
hotel famous for honeymooners.
"Gee, Rio sounds great," I said, "but...
I want to marry at Highland Baptist...
long white veil...parents and friends...
your wings and dress uniform...
But first, I want my own flying career."

I was a *liberated woman* in 45's Big Apple.
Then my love returned home from the wars.
That shortened the *liberated woman's* career.
After four months—she wore a long white veil
After forty years—Mal flew her to Rio.

Black Lace, 1945

Mama was getting me ready for my New Orleans honeymoon. She didn't give advice; she just sewed nightgowns like crazy. Her feet rocked faster and faster on the worn treadle of her carved-oak wrought-iron Singer sewing machine.

Oh, the dreams Mama and I shared over the years. Easy as designing dresses for paper dolls, I drew sketches of off-the-shoulder ruffled evening gowns. Mama, with that sorcerer of a Singer, made my dreams come true.

My gauzy be-ribboned white gown, like new-fallen snow, was perfect for the first night. For later nights, I'd wear pastel gowns, like sweet-scented flower petals. The gown Mama had just finished was black satin with a peek-a-book lace top—seductive with my long black hair.

As I paraded around Mama's sewing room in this alluring creation, I could imagine my honeymoon: swinging open the bathroom door, as I posed in this black wicked vision. I could hear his hot and heavy breathing.

As Margaret, my older married sister watched my posturing, she teased, "But primping takes you so long, by the time you make your grand entrance, poor Mal will be sound asleep." As Mama put the spool back in the thread drawer, she laughed and laughed at Margaret's foolishness.

The white gown worked well on the first night at the Tutwiler Hotel, in our hometown of Birmingham. The next day Mal drove us to the St. Charles in New Orleans, where the *real* honeymoon would begin.

During the long ride south down U.S. 31, I had time to doze and dream. I knew it was perfectly logical to wear the pastel gowns after the white one, leaving the black one for the last night of the honeymoon. On the other hand, I decided the black lace would be perfect for launching a honeymoon in this city *renowned* for honeymooning. Besides, I couldn't wait.

Mal took a quick shower, slid into his tailored burgundy pajamas, leaving the sleek marble bathroom to me. After soaking in bubble bath, lathering each limb, giving my hair the required hundred strokes, dusting my special places with Wild Lilac bath powder, and touching my left ear lobe with a drop of Evening In Paris perfume...
I swung open the bathroom door for my grand entrance.

My heavens! He was asleep. Margaret's prediction had come true. His arms and legs were sprawled, pajamas awry, mouth open. I heard hot and heavy breathing, but not the kind I longed for. The black nightgown and I crept into bed, crying ourselves to sleep.

Fifty years later Mal said, "But Hon, it's a long hard drive from Birmingham to New Orleans."
That may be so, but even after fifty years, I still haven't forgiven him.

Ain't Dead Yet

Mal adores his Granny Mam.
On our honeymoon
at the St. Charles
I take the phone from his hand,
"Looking forward to meeting you Mam
Heard so much about you."

"You'll find a mighty sassy Mam,"
she says.

I knew the legends—
flowered hats
hair and nails done Fridays
poker games Saturdays
silver flask in purse
to shock teetotalers.

Sumptuous dinner
antique china and silver
"I tell 'em don't finger my stuff
I ain't dead yet."

Riding back to the hotel she confided,
"They sent me your picture.
Too persnickety.
Told 'em I wouldn't like you,
but I do"

Back home in Memphis
the family demitasse spoons arrive.
Card scrawled
in peacock-blue-ink—
"Ain't dead yet!"

New Orleans, 1945

Mam's House

Mam had a weakness
for her grandson, Jim,
but wouldn't allow herself
to be an easy mark.

Jim, a student at Tulane,
brought his dates to Mam's house,
knowing her hair
would be in soft curls,
nails tinted blush pink.

They gobbled her sugar cookies.
She made them again.
Hid them again.
They stole them again.

Sunday, three a.m.
she answered the door
seeing Jim's glazed eyes,
his tux awry,
"I can't go home Mam."

"Not coming here neither.
Never could stand a man
couldn't hold his liquor.
The night's right nippy
but sleep it off on the swing."

She left. Returned.
She hit him with a pillow.
She hit him with a quilt.

"Young man!
I sure hope you're feeling
a right smart-of-guilt."

Daddy, My First Love

Being youngest
I've often heard him say
"The baby of a family is special."

At three
I wanted to marry him.
I later found another.

Daddy never told me
he loved me,

Through the years
I basked
in the warmth
of his unspoken love.

Now I've come full circle
with my first love
as he cuddles my first born.

This wee one
has brought us together
in a very special way.

Memphis, Tennessee, 1948

Shadow

Monkeyshines

Mama's doing errands
Buddy's looking out for me.

Like one monkey
grooming another
he and Jace Green
cut each other's hair
snickering as they pocket
two bits for hair-cut-money.

"Leaving, Dinky
You need anything
call this number."
Only Buddy calls me Dinky.

Shortly I need something
265-7000
Rrrrrring:
"Police Department."

Bessemer, Alabama, 1929

Paper Route, 1932

I stood in awe of everything
my big brother, Buddy, did,
even to his calling me Dinky.
Mr. Schelessi paid him
with stuff from his store—
black and red licorice sticks
jawbreakers black cows moon pies.
Buddy stashed this exotic stuff
but I rarely got a glimpse of it.

Sunday 3 a.m. Clock's alarm jammed.
Buddy figured it was too late
to pedal papers by bike.
He'd have to borrow Dad's new Chevy.
Parking atop 19th Street hill
to deliver an apartment house
he forgot to set the brake.
He chased the car all the way
down the hill until it crashed
into Mr. Beaver's great oak tree.

Just before dawn Buddy parked
the smashed car back in the garage
neatly leaning the bumper
against the garage wall,
then went to sleep.

Stomping upstairs from the garage
in her church clothes
Mama flapped her arms over Buddy's bed
like a Baptist preacher at revival time.
"Sleeping! How dare you
when you've wrecked
our beautiful new Chevrolet."

Dad stalked close behind like
an usher with the collection plate,
"You'll work at the steel mill
to pay the repair bill.
No summer camp this year."

I remembered
his box of blue ribbons
from Camp Cosby.

After Buddy's baptism under fire,
watching the ordained ones stride out,
I settled at the foot of his bed.
He stared frowning at the bed covers
for a long minute
then reached for the brown paper bag
in his night table drawer—
"Here, Dinky."
He shared
his licorice sticks with me.

The Doll House

At Auburn University, during the Depression, when Aunt Luckie and Uncle Red were bride and groom, he built a little eat-shop called "The Doll House," where they served short order food to the college kids. The little house had two dormer windows, and four columns holding an open porch. Flanking the entrance were window boxes over-flowing with petunias.

Buddy, my big brother—a good student and handsome to boot—worked there in the summers during his high school days. Nestled in the center of town, "The Doll House" was leased in 1961 to a walk-up ice cream shop—"SaniFreeze." The college kids called it "The Flush."

Later, "Save-The-Flush" signs sprang up on campus. Students rebelled because "The Flush" was going down, so AmSouth Bank could go up. The Auburn Gazette pictured "The Doll House" as it stood since 1939. "They don't realize what this landmark means to Auburn," students howled.

The story didn't mention Uncle Red (long gone) or Aunt Luckie, who's in an Auburn nursing home. Nobody remembers Buddy's black curly hair. He too is gone—buried at Arlington Cemetery.

Most Wanted: Our Buddy

Duke, Tulane, Alabama, Auburn—
all Dixieland knocked at our door
to induce our Buddy to play football.
At 12, I secretly held him as hero,
and enjoyed the flourish and frenzy.

Dad's eyes brightened
when they fell on his only son—
Pegasus
winging
his way toward the stars.

Colonel McIntyre,
a regal, sharp-eyed eagle,
scouting for Georgetown U.
wined and dined Buddy—
introduced him to hilarious
merriment at Mardi Gras.

The Colonel gave Dad his pledge,
"Four years education guaranteed,
even if, God forbid
your son should become
a football casualty."

Mama looked as amused and amazed
as a kitten unraveling string,
when Baptist Deacon Daddy
chose a Catholic university.

“It sounded,” Buddy said,
“like the crack of a bat.”
At the first college practice,
like a falling sapling,
Buddy splintered his knee.

“His 4 years at Georgetown,” Dad said,
“will no longer be that of a hero
in his own Southern town.
He’ll never play football again.”

Washington, D.C.

Details

Mama sensed a quiet glow—
she loved
Buddy's betrothed.

He confided
"Fran's a Catholic"
He paused
"She's been married."

Mama thought
of Baptist Deacon Daddy.
Looking up into Buddy's face
deep into his eyes
she went back to baking
spicy apple pies.

"Let's not bother
Daddy
with details."

Bessemer, 1951

Home In Cuernavaca

After retiring
from career marine service
to the land of eternal spring
Buddy and Fran built
a guest house
for Mama and Daddy—
a downy nest
for living out their days

Mama chirped
"They can't speak a word
of English down here
I can't understand TV
Miss my friends"

Like a couple
of homing pigeons
they winged their way
back to Alabama
and Highland Baptist
where they sang

"How great Thou art"

Cuernavaca, Mexico, 1961

Call Of The Woods

As he listens
to the call
of the woods,
Dad's eyes shine
like the barrel
of his shotgun,

his boots crunching
autumn leaves,
his instincts sure
as a hound dog's
howl.

At twilight
he walks up
the back path
birds in hand,
looking as peaceful
as a strong oak
after a shower.

1930

Shadow

Dad presents his favorite
hunting rifle
as a parting gift.
"I want you to enjoy it, Son.
I'm too old for hunting."

After years of service
over most of the world
as a career Marine,
Buddy and Fran leave Alabama
to begin retirement
in Cuernavaca.

In Mexico, Fran grooms white
bougainvillaea
climbing stucco garden walls.
She hovers over dahlia and daisy
like a golden monarch.
She hums, relaxed, content,
confident the move will cure
her husband's lingering
depression.

Buddy and Fran are childless,
but in their lighted pool
Buddy swims each evening
with Shadow,
his loyal-large-black poodle,
whom he loves as an only child.

Lightning strikes.
Shadow whimpers.
Licks Buddy's wounds.
Hovers over the body
like a cloud of black fog.

Fran's tear-tarnished voice
reaches Alabama,

"Daddy, Buddy's dead
Shot himself
Yes, Dad—
Oh God! With your rifle."

1965

A Marine's Last March

White crosses like white doves
flying formation
above vibrant manicured green

Buddy's flag-draped coffin
Smartly uniformed marines step-
ping to drum rolls

Riderless roan horse (boots turned backward)
followed by Fran's black veil

Gaping grave site
Thunderous 21-gun-salute
Taps echoing farewell to

Col. Walter Holomon
USMC
1917-1962

Arlington Cemetery
Washington, D.C., 1962

Father And Son

Learning of his only son's death
by his own hand
Dad slumped over
like an aged warrior
suffering a direct hit.

In Daddy's den, dominating
the wall over the fireplace
hung an oil portrait of Buddy,
splendid in his Colonel's uniform.
Medals bright. Eyes gentle.

Each day during anxious years
Dad followed the war on wall maps.
Finally, his sleepless nights ended.
Thanking God for the safe return
the father hugged his marine.

After the final separation,
for the remainder of the old man's life
the son's gentle eyes
looked out from the large portrait lit
by flickering flames.
The father sat before him
in his easy chair.

One man as silent as the other.

1962

Letting Go

Old Gray Hat

As an old man
in his recliner-chair
Daddy wore
the sporty new clothes
I bought him
(to please Mama and me).

Lifted
his old hat
from the hall tree
for our daily walks
together.

Like Old Times

At Hamlet Care Center
holding his hand
Mama said to Daddy,

"It's almost time
for my ride."
"You can drive yourself."
"Not any more. I'm too old
to drive."
"Lie beside me, Hazel.
You can stay here with me."

She nestled against him
in his hospital bed.

Daddy, Feeble

His cloudy eyes
reckon
strange reckonings,
oblivious to fruits
of his orchard.

Like a ghosted
Southern town
riddled by ribbons
of fractured concrete,
play yards
long silenced by inertia
cobwebs, mold.

Like a Southern town
once bustling with dignity,
whose empty buildings
are separated
from their souls.

1975

Letting Go

For fifty years
Daddy sang bass
at Highland Baptist.

At ninety-four
at Hamlet Care Center
he sat up
in his hospital bed
singing
The Old Rugged Cross.
"This is some church!"
he said.

Nurse Rachel
smiled at me.
"He's okay
but it's breaking
your mama's heart."

Mama said
"He won't go
till I let him go."

So she did.

Bessemer, Alabama, 1977

Ruffles

In her prime Mama said,
"Now-a-days rrruffles
are all the rage."
Taking a pin from her mouth,
"If yours ain't the spit-n-image
of my figure at your age!"

I can still hear
the palpitation of the treadle,
the whispering whirl of the wheel,
and a lively snap of ruby red thread.
Out came lacy ruffles enough
to turn a couturier's head.

During her last days,
an old lady of 86
in her dainty pink night gown,
Mama said,
"I miss sewing most of all.
Ann,
thread
my needle."

Ponte Vedra Beach, Florida, 1980

Mama's Choice

Mama never feared death.
She feared
nursing homes.

She kissed
Daddy's cold forehead
whispering,
"I'll be along soon."

In time, Mama entered
Jax Care Center.
She shrugged,
"Never mind."

In a matter of days
her spirit soared

at last,
to be with Daddy.

Lights Out

Mama smoothed a spot
on her bed,
"Sit beside me, Ann."

I said, "I forgot to turn
my car lights out, Mama.
I'll be right back."

The moment was lost forever.
We never
said goodbye.

Jacksonville, Florida, 1981

The Diamond Ring

I feel closest to Mama,
when I gaze into the diamond
solitaire on my finger.
How many times had I seen her
tenderly rotate the stone
just to watch the fire within.
This was the engagement
ring she received at eighteen.

The pleasure she felt wearing
the ring and capturing the heart
of "Mr. Holomon" remained
throughout her life.
She wore it until her last breath,
then as she had promised
it went to the eldest daughter.
It looked elegant on Margaret's finger.

She cherished it for years, then
on her eighty seventh birthday:
"Ann, I want you to have Mama's ring.
It would please her for you to wear it."
Gently, she rotated the stone,
then slipped it off her finger.
"It's always been in my will
but I want you to have it now."

A young friend asked her, "How
can you give up your beautiful ring?"
Margaret looked up slowly:
"Some day you'll understand."

God's Reflection

When I was young
I longed
to see the fullness
of God's Face.

I searched.

When I gaze
into the power of the sun,
I am blinded
by its brilliance.

While His glory passes
oak trees bow,
magnolias impart
their fragrance.

I'm content
to watch golden leaves
glistening in the breeze.
They mirror His splendor.

God's reflection
is the essence of family.
Now I understand.

Family Secrets

Aunt Mildred's Cakes

The Cake Lady

Friends and family far and wide declared Aunt Mildred's three famous cakes to be the best in all the South. She was known as the Cake Lady. Members of the community who fell ill, had a death in the family, or had reason to feel sad were sure to receive a cake. Sometimes she would cut one into generous slices to take to a nursing home, where they'd eat, laugh, and have a party together.

Also, for Aunt Mildred, each event was cause for celebration. Every few days she would make a cake for a birthday, anniversary, wedding or because our clan was gathering. "Which kind would you like?" she'd ask, "my Sour Cream Pound Cake, Devil's Food Pound Cake or Fresh-Apple-and-Nut Cake?" Hearing the names would make our mouths water.

She'd say to one of us, "Honey, heat up my coffee cup. I like my men and my coffee hot." She'd laugh and we'd laugh. Those days were filled with laughter. Her eyes would brighten as we finished off her home-churned peach ice cream, along with a generous slice of her Sour Cream Pound Cake.

Aunt Mildred's Fresh-Apple and Nut Cake

3 eggs
1 1/4 cup Wesson Oil
3 cups flour
Mix: 1 cup white sugar
 1 cup dark brown sugar
Mix: 3 cups chopped apples
 1 cup chopped nuts
1 teaspoon soda
1 teaspoon cinnamon
1/4 teaspoon salt
2 teaspoon vanilla

Beat eggs well
Add mixed sugars
Add oil and vanilla, gradually
Add sifted dry ingredients slowly
Add chopped apples & nuts (mixed)

Bake in tubed pan 1 hour, 15 minutes

Aunt Mildred's Sour Cream Pound Cake

2 sticks butter
3 cups sugar
6 large eggs
3 cups cake flour
1/4 teaspoon soda
1 8-ounce carton sour cream
3 teaspoons extract
(vanilla or lemon or mix them)

Get butter to room temperature, then beat
Add sugar gradually
Add eggs one at a time
(Beat well after each one)
Add flour/soda and sour cream, alternately
Add extract.

Cook at 325 degrees for 1 hour 15 minutes.

Aunt Mildred's Devil's Food Pound Cake

2 sticks butter
1/2 cup Crisco
3 cups sugar
5 eggs
3 cups cake flour + 1/2 cup cocoa
1/2 teaspoon baking powder
1/4 teaspoon salt
1 cup milk
2 teaspoons vanilla

Cream butter and Crisco (room temperature)
Add sugar gradually.
Add eggs, one at a time,
beating after each addition.

Add dry ingredients, (sifted together)

alternately with milk and vanilla.
Put in greased floured cake pan

Cook at 325 degrees for 1 hour 15 minutes.

She says, "This makes too much for a cake pan, so I make a small one with left-over batter. I bake it in my toaster oven. I use any smaller pan I may have, or sometimes I make muffins with the left over mix. I get to test the big cake by eating my little cake."

* * *

Happy Feasting!

To order additional copies of ***Family Secrets***, complete the information below.

Ship to: (please print)

Name ______________________________

Address ______________________________

City, State, Zip ______________________________

Day phone ______________________________

_____ copies of ***Family Secrets*** @ $10.00 each $ ________

Postage and handling @ $1.50 per book $ ________

Fla. residents add 6% tax $ ________

Total amount enclosed $ ________

Make checks payable to *Ann Sims*

Send to: 9449 Preston Trail West

Ponte Vedra Beach, FL 32082

Proceeds will be given to mental health associations, & local charity bazaars.

With this coupon, price per book is $10.00
(including shipping, handling and tax).

- -

To order additional copies of ***Family Secrets***, complete the information below.

Ship to: (please print)

Name ______________________________

Address ______________________________

City, State, Zip ______________________________

Day phone ______________________________

_____ copies of ***Family Secrets*** @ $10.00 each $ ________

Postage and handling @ $1.50 per book $ ________

Fla. residents add 6% tax $ ________

Total amount enclosed $ ________

Make checks payable to *Ann Sims*

Send to: 9449 Preston Trail West

Ponte Vedra Beach, FL 32082

Proceeds will be given to mental health associations, & local charity bazaars.

With this coupon, price per book is $10.00
(including shipping, handling and tax).